Holiday Freezer Cooking from 30 Day Gourmet

Index

30 DAY GOURMET
HELPFUL HINTS AND TIPS

TIMING IS EVERYTHING! There are as many different ways to use this cookbook as there are holiday cooks! Look at your own schedule and decide which parts of the meal you need to assemble early and when you will have the time. 10-12 of these recipes could be done in one 8-hour day. But if you don't have a whole day, try starting early and doing 2-3 recipes per week. With the exception of the raw dough, everything in this cookbook can be made at least a month ahead of time and frozen. Many can stay frozen much longer.

CASUAL GATHERINGS: With the exception of the *Raspberry Fruit Dip, Carrots with Cashew Butter*, pie fillings, and beverage recipe, our holiday recipes can be frozen in disposable foil pans. Purchase pans similar in size to the ones called for in the recipes. Follow the assembly directions as stated, but skip the freezer bag. Cover the foil pans with freezer weight or heavy-duty aluminum foil (crimping around edges of pans tightly), or slide the pans into freezer bags. Remove the excess air, and freeze. Instead of placing the thawed contents into another baking dish, just bake it right in the pan. Easy serving with less clean up!

LARGE GATHERINGS: Suggest that each family attending be in charge of one of the recipes. If each family makes enough of their recipe to serve everyone, less work is done by all. The more expensive dishes may be divided between two or more families if you wish.

CHILDREN: Holiday gatherings can be tough on the little ones. If the meal is scheduled at an odd time, don't make them starve before the meal – it will only make them grouchy and less pleasant to dine with. A few crackers, a slice of cheese, and pieces of fruit may keep their energy and mood from waning beyond the possibility of being civil at the table. Children don't always like holiday foods. If they only see these foods once a year, they may be a little less than enthused about sampling 20 strange looking things on their plates. Don't expect more than they can give. Compromise is not a bad word at the holidays – the goal here is a *happy* holiday.

THAWING: Foods will reheat or cook more quickly and evenly if they start at room temperature. After thawing, they can be left at room temperature up to, but not more than, two hours. Do not leave any perishables out at room temperature longer than two hours.

ON HAND INGREDIENTS: Here's a tip for the things that are not in your freezer that you have planned for the meal, like butter, jelly, ice, whipped topping, etc. Mark the packages or cans with a big black X with a permanent marker. This will keep you from inadvertently using them up before the big day.

SERVINGS: Our recipes are based on standard adult servings. If you expect your guests to eat two helpings, you should consider using a larger quantity of that recipe.

TALKING TURKEY: Many people are intimidated by this popular holiday fowl. Most of us have at one time or another feasted on a tough, dried out turkey. This won't happen to your poor bird if you have the right information. Be wary of advice from friends or relatives. Aunt Lou Lou's secret recipe may not be safe. We encourage all would-be bird cookers to contact the USDA's Meat and Poultry Hotline. Their toll free number is 800-535-4555. They will give you all the advice you need over the telephone, or you can request free printed materials. They will send a whole packet of information to your door free of charge.

30 DAY GOURMET • HOLIDAY COOKING • TALLY SHEET

1. Write the name of your first recipe in line 1.
2. In the diagonal columns, fill in the needed ingredients for that recipe.
3. Going horizontally across line 1, fill in the appropriate amounts of each ingredient for that recipe.
4. Repeat this procedure for each recipe.

5. Be sure to account for any needed freezer bags or containers, spray oils, etc...needed for each recipe.
6. After all ingredients and packaging needs are accounted for, total the amount needed of each recipe at the bottom of each column.
7. Under the "total needed" boxes write in

the amount of each ingredient that you already have in your cabinets, freezer, pantry or refrigerator.
8. Subtract the "on hand" amount from the "total needed" amount and put that number in the "total to buy" boxes.
9. Transfer the "total to buy" amounts to the Shopping List on the back of this sheet.

Food Type / Recipe Title	Meats	Frozen Produce	Fresh Produce	Grains, Pasta & Doughs	Dairy	Canned Food Items	Spices	Misc.	Packaging
1.									
2.									
3.									
4.									
5.									
6.									
7.									
8.									
9.									
10.									
11.									
12.									
13.									
14.									
15.									
16.									
17.									
18.									
19.									
20.									
21.									
Total Needed									
- Total on Hand									
= Total to Buy									

30 DAY GOURMET
SHOPPING LIST

Beef	Canned Foods	Frozen Produce	Spices
_____	_____	_____	_____
_____	_____	_____	_____
_____	_____	_____	_____
_____	_____	_____	_____
_____	_____	_____	_____
Chicken	_____	_____	_____
_____	_____	_____	_____
_____	_____	_____	_____
_____	_____	_____	_____
_____	_____	_____	_____
Turkey	_____	**Fresh Produce**	_____
_____	_____	_____	_____
_____	_____	_____	_____
_____	_____	_____	_____
_____	_____	_____	**Miscellaneous**
Pork	**Grains**	_____	_____
_____	_____	_____	_____
_____	_____	_____	_____
_____	_____	_____	_____
Fish	_____	**Staples**	_____
_____	**Pasta**	_____	_____
_____	_____	_____	_____
Dairy	_____	_____	_____
_____	**Breads**	_____	_____
_____	_____	_____	_____
_____	_____	_____	_____
_____	_____	_____	_____
_____	_____	_____	_____
_____	**Dry Beans**	_____	_____
_____	_____	_____	_____
_____	_____	_____	_____
_____	_____	_____	_____

COUNTDOWN SHEET

MEAL EVENT _____   LOCATION _____   TIME SCHEDULED _____

NAME OF RECIPE	Date/Time place in refrigerator	Date/Time set at room temperature	Heating/Cooking Container	Heating/Cooking Source	Start time to Heat/cook	Temperature or power	Serving container/dish

FREEZER PACKAGING TIPS

There are several different options to choose from when deciding what kind of packaging to use for freezing these recipes. Some are disposable, some are not. The convenience factor may outweigh the cost factor depending on your situation for the holiday event. We always suggest that you freeze in thin layers or shallow containers. The food will freeze and thaw more quickly and evenly.

ZIP TOP FREEZER BAGS:

These disposable containers have become our favorites for most situations because of their relative low cost and convenience. Freezer bags also travel well in a cooler if you are transporting your food to a party destination. Make sure you purchase quality freezer bags, not food storage bags. You get what you pay for in most instances. Label them with a sharp point permanent marker before filling. They are not only hard to write on when full, but the marker will not work on a cold, warm, or wet bag. We find it very convenient to write the cooking directions right on the bag. This keeps us from having to look up a recipe card or page in a book in order to cook the food. Of course in this book you also have the countdown sheet to help you.

Cool foods thoroughly before filling the bags. To keep the outside of the bag from getting messy, cuff the top of the bag to the outside a couple of inches. Fill the bags with food, then remove the excess air. There are a couple of ways to remove the air. For most soft, liquid, or smooth textured foods, seal the bag to within one inch of the end. Hold the bag so that the open end of the seal is at the top, and the rest of the bag is below it, like a diamond shape. With your free hand, carefully press the air from the bottom of the bag up, forcing it out the opening. When as much of the air is expelled as possible, complete the seal.

Another method that we like for recipes that must be frozen in pans is to place the pan in a freezer bag, insert a drinking straw into one corner of the seal, zip the bag up tightly against the straw and suck the air out. You have to keep holding the seal while you suck out the air. When the air is depleted, keep holding the seal tight against the straw while pulling the straw out. As the bottom of the straw comes out, finish sealing the bag.

If you don't want to tie all your pans up in the refrigerator, here is another option. Line your pans with good quality plastic wrap or foil. Coat with cooking oil spray, then assemble the recipe as directed. Place the pan of food, uncovered, into the freezer. As soon as the food is firmly frozen, pop the block of food out, and place it inside a freezer bag. Remove the excess air, seal and freeze. To use this frozen block, unwrap it while it is still frozen. If you have any difficulty removing the wrap, run the bottom of it briefly under warm water until it comes loose. Place the frozen block of food in its original pan, cover with plastic wrap, foil, or a lid, and thaw as usual.

For recipes requiring more than one container, like the *Carrots with Cashew Butter*, you might try placing both components into one large bag. This keeps the parts together and keeps them from getting lost in the bottom of the freezer.

RIGID PLASTIC CONTAINERS:

These work well for recipes that are more fragile, like pie crusts, dinner rolls, potato rosettes, and the frozen salads. Please use freezer containers and not recycled plastic tubs. If there is much air separating the food from the container's seal, you can cover the surface of the food with a layer of plastic wrap. This will keep ice crystals from forming on the surface. If you use a freezer container for recipes with much liquid, like gravy or broth, allow enough room for expansion during freezing. A good rule of thumb is to allow a ½ inch at the top of a freezer container. These containers travel well.

FOIL PANS:

Foil pans are fine for informal gatherings, potlucks, etc. They can often be slid into a freezer bag, or you can seal them with heavy-duty foil wrap. Make sure to crimp it tightly onto the edges of the pans. If you have adequate freezer space and you can afford to do so, freezing many of your foods this way is very convenient. These containers travel well, however, they may need to be supported by a tray.

FREEZING IN SERVING DISHES:

Make sure that the dishes are freezer and heat safe. If possible, slide the dishes into freezer bags. If they are too large, you can wrap them with foil, making sure to seal well. If the dishes are glass or ceramic, make sure the frozen dish is not set on a hot surface when removed from the freezer. You may shatter your dish! These do not always travel well. Place the dish in a cardboard box and pad the sides with towels.

Recipe: Dorothy's Butterscotch Breakfast Rolls

Serves:	24 rolls	48 rolls	72 rolls	96 rolls	120 rolls	144 rolls
Ingredients:						
Frozen dinner roll dough, 25 oz. pkg.	1	2	3	4	5	6
Non-instant butterscotch 3.5 oz. pudding mix	1	2	3	4	5	6
Brown sugar, packed	½ C.	1 C.	1 ½ C.	2 C.	2 ½ C.	3 C.
Cinnamon	1 t.	2 t.	1 T.	1 T. + 1 t.	1 T. + 2 t.	2 T.
Walnuts or pecans, chopped	1 C.	2 C.	3 C.	4 C.	5 C.	6 C.
Butter/margarine	½ C.	1 C.	1½ C.	2 C.	2½ C.	3 C.

This recipe can be combined the night before your holiday, left in the refrigerator and then served after baking. OR you can combine and bake the rolls, freeze them and just reheat to serve. Both ways are yummy!

Assembly Directions: Grease two 8 or 9 inch round cake or pie pans for each recipe. Put 12 frozen dough balls in each pan. Combine the pudding mix, brown sugar, and cinnamon in a small bowl. Sprinkle evenly over the frozen dough. Sprinkle with the chopped nuts (optional). Melt the butter and pour evenly over the pans of dough. Cover pans loosely with plastic wrap and allow to dough to rise at room temperature 6 hours or in the refrigerator overnight. When the dough is through rising, bake in a 375° preheated oven for 15 minutes.

To serve now: Invert the pans immediately onto large heatproof plates.

To freeze now and serve later: Allow rolls to cool in the pan then place cooled pans in labeled one-gallon freezer bags. Remove excess air, seal and freeze. To serve frozen rolls, thaw them in the pan completely, then place in a 400° oven for 10 minutes. Invert immediately onto heatproof plates and serve.

Comments: Try this with vanilla flavored pudding instead – very good! If you would prefer to use homemade dough, our Easy No Knead Potato Roll dough is excellent in this recipe. Use half of a single recipe of the potato dough to make twenty-four walnut sized balls. Freeze them on a waxed paper or plastic wrap lined pan. Freeze balls of dough solid, then use as above.

Storage Time:
Baked: Refrigerator (40°): 4-6 days, Freezer: 12-15 months
Unbaked: Refrigerator (40°): 6-8 hours, Freezer: 2 weeks

Recipe: Bread Pudding Muffins

Quantity:	12	24	36	48	60	72
Ingredients:						
Milk	1 ½ C.	3 C.	4½ C.	6 C.	7½ C.	9 C.
Eggs	2	4	6	8	10	12
Brown sugar, packed	¼ C.	½ C.	¾ C.	1 C.	1¼ C.	1 ½ C.
Cinnamon	1 T.	2T.	3T.	¼ C.	¼C.+ 1T.	¼C. + 2T.
Vanilla extract	1 T.	2T.	3T.	¼ C.	¼C.+ 1T.	¼C. + 2T.
Butter/Margarine, melted	2 T.	¼ C.	¼C. + 2T	½ C.	½C. + 2T	¾ C.
Raisins (optional)	2/3 C.	1 1/3 C.	2 C.	2 2/3 C.	3 1/3 C.	4 C.
Bread slices, cut in ½"cubes	12	24	36	48	60	72

Assembly Directions: In a large mixing bowl, combine by hand all ingredients except raisins and bread cubes, mixing well. Add bread cubes and raisins (optional). Toss with a spoon to coat well.

Freezing Directions:

Option 1: Pour entire mixture into a labeled one-gallon freezer bag. Remove excess air, seal and freeze.

Option 2: Spoon mixture evenly into a muffin tin(s) that has been coated with spray pan coating. Cover pan with plastic wrap, then slide into a labeled two gallon freezer bag. Remove excess air, seal and freeze.

To serve:

Option 1: Thaw bag of muffin mixture and spoon into a muffin tin(s). Bake in a 350° preheated oven for 35 or 40 minutes until well browned on top. Remove from tin and cool muffins on a wire rack.

Option 2: If frozen in the tin, thaw completely, then bake as above. The muffins may also be baked as above, then frozen and reheated at 350° for 10 minutes.

Comments: Whole wheat, white, French, or cinnamon breads can be used in this recipe. For a richer recipe use cream, or evaporated skim milk to replace the milk.

Lower Fat Options: Use skim milk. Use two egg whites to replace each egg.

Storage Time:
Baked: Refrigerator (40°): 4-6 days, Freezer: 2-4 months
Unbaked: Refrigerator (40°): 2-4 days, Freezer: 1-2 months

Recipe: Breakfast Egg Casserole

Servings:	6	12	18	24	30	36
Ingredients:						
Bread slices, crust removed if desired, make 1" cubes	8	16	24	32	40	48
Ham, diced	4 oz.	8 oz.	12 oz.	16 oz.	20 oz.	24 oz.
Swiss cheese, shredded	4 oz.	8 oz.	12 oz.	16 oz.	20 oz.	24 oz.
Cheddar cheese, shredded	4 oz.	8 oz.	12 oz.	16 oz.	20 oz.	24 oz.
Eggs	3	6	9	12	15	18
Milk	1 C.	2 C.	3 C.	4 C.	5 C.	6 C.
Onion powder	$\frac{1}{4}$ t.	$\frac{1}{2}$ t.	$\frac{3}{4}$ t.	1 t.	$1\frac{1}{4}$ t.	$1\frac{1}{2}$ t.
Salt	$\frac{1}{2}$ t.	1 t.	$1\frac{1}{2}$ t.	2 t.	$2\frac{1}{2}$ t.	1 T.
Dry mustard	$\frac{1}{2}$ t.	1 t.	$1\frac{1}{2}$ t.	2 t.	$2\frac{1}{2}$ t.	1 T.

Assembly Directions: Place $\frac{1}{2}$ the bread cubes, in a greased 9" square or round baking pan, or other heatproof baking dish. Over the bread cubes, layer half of the diced ham and half of each shredded cheese. Repeat all the layers ending with a layer of cheese. The pan will be very full. Beat the remaining ingredients together and pour over the pan. Cover the pan loosely with plastic wrap and refrigerate overnight if serving the next day. If not, continue with freezing instructions.

Freezing Directions: Cover the pan loosely with plastic wrap and place inside a labeled one-gallon freezer bag. Remove excess air from the bag, seal and freeze.

To Serve: Thaw the pan in the refrigerator for about 12 to 14 hours. Remove from bag and discard plastic wrap. Bake in a 375° preheated oven for 35 – 40 minutes. Cool 5-10 minutes before slicing to serve.

Comments: The doubled recipe will fill a 9x13" baking pan and serve 12 – 14. The casserole may be baked frozen. Bake it at 300° for 25 minutes, then 350° for 35 minutes. A half-pound of bacon or sausage, cooked, drained and crumbled may be substituted for the ham. A cup of sliced summer sausage, or similar sausage may also be substituted. A small can of drained shrimp or crab would also be good in this. A cup of cooked diced broccoli, fresh or canned mushrooms, or sweet bell pepper may be added.

Lower Fat Options: Any of the reduced fat cheeses can be used, just don't expect them to melt the same. There are many reduced fat ham products, including turkey hams. Reduced fat summer sausages and turkey bacon products also work well.

Storage Time: Baked or Unbaked: Refrigerator (40°): 2-4 days, Freezer: 1-2 months

Recipe: Cranberry Breakfast Cobbler

Serves:	6	12	18	24	30	36
Ingredients:						
Butter/margarine, softened	2 T	4 T.	6 T.	8 T.	10 T.	12 T.
Cranberries, fresh or thawed, rinsed and dried	1½ C.	3 C.	4½ C.	6 C.	7½ C.	9 C.
Walnuts, chopped	¾ C.	1½ C.	2¼ C.	3 C.	3¾ C.	4½ C.
Brown sugar, packed	1/3 C.	2/3 C.	1 C.	1 1/3 C.	1 2/3 C.	2 C.
Eggs	1	2	3	4	5	6
Sugar	½ C.	1 C.	1½ C.	2 C.	2½ C.	3 C.
Flour	½ C.	1 C.	1½ C.	2 C.	2½ C.	3 C.
Butter, melted and cooled	6 T.	12 T.	18 T.	24 T.	32 T.	40 T.
Vanilla extract	½ t.	1 t.	1½ t.	2 t.	2½ t.	1 T.

Assembly Directions: Grease an 8 or 9 inch round cake pan with the softened butter, using it all. Place the cranberries in a single layer in the bottom of the pan. Sprinkle the nuts over the berries, then sprinkle the brown sugar over all. In a medium mixing bowl, beat egg, sugar, flour, melted butter, and vanilla extract until smooth. Spoon the batter over the cranberry layer. Bake at 375° for 40 – 50 minutes, until browned and a toothpick inserted in the cake layer comes out clean and dry. Cool on a wire rack. When cool, cut around the outside edges with a knife to loosen.

Freezing Directions: Place the cooled pan in a labeled one-gallon freezer bag. Remove excess air, seal and freeze.

To Serve: Thaw cobbler completely. Serve cold or reheat for 10 – 15 minutes at 375°. Serve from the pan, or invert hot cobbler onto a serving plate. If any of the cranberry mixture sticks to the pan, scrape it off with a spatula and spread it onto the place it came from on the cobbler.

Lower Fat Options: Replace the cake batter (eggs, sugar, flour, butter, and vanilla extract) with a recipe of our fat free cobbler mix from *The Freezer Cooking Manual from 30 Day Gourmet: A Month of Meals Made Easy.*

Storage Time: Refrigerator (40°): 4-6 days, Freezer: 2-3 months

Recipe: Raspberry Fruit Dip

Serves:	6	12	18	24	30	36
Quantity:	3 C.	6 C.	9 C.	12 C.	15 C.	18 C.
Ingredients:						
Fresh or frozen raspberries	1 ½ C.	3 C.	4½ C.	6 C.	7½ C.	9 C.
Sugar	1/3 C.	2/3 C.	1 C.	1 1/3 C.	1 2/3 C.	2 C.
Ricotta cheese	1 C.	2 C.	3 C.	4 C.	5 C.	6 C.
Cream cheese	8 oz.	16 oz.	24 oz.	32 oz.	40 oz.	48 oz.
Lemon juice	2 T.	¼ C.	¼ C. + 2T.	½ C.	½ C. + 2 T.	¾ C.
Vanilla extract	1 t.	2 t.	1 T.	1 T. + 1 t.	1 T. + 2 t.	2 T.

Assembly and Freezing Directions: Combine all the ingredients in a food processor or blender and puree until smooth. Pour mixture into a labeled freezer bag or container. Remove excess air, seal and freeze.

To Serve: Thaw mixture and stir well. Serve with seasonally available fresh fruit.

Comments: This also makes a great fruit salad dressing.

Lower Fat Options: Use reduced fat ricotta cheese and lower or fat free cream cheese or Neufchatel.

Storage Time: Refrigerator (40°): 3-4 days, Freezer: 3 months

Recipe: Dijon Turkey Spread

Serves:	6	12	18	24	30	36
Quantity:	2½ C.	5 C.	7½ C.	10 C.	12½ C.	15 C.
Ingredients:						
Sour cream	8 oz.	16 oz.	24 oz.	32 oz.	40 oz.	48 oz.
Cream cheese	4 oz.	8 oz.	12 oz.	16 oz.	20 oz.	24 oz.
Dijon mustard	2 T.	¼ C.	¼ C. + 2 T.	½ C.	½ C. + 2 T.	¾ C.
Garlic powder	¼ t.	½ t.	¾ t.	1 t.	1¼ t.	1½ t.
Turkey breast, cooked and diced	1 C	2 C.	3 C.	4 C.	5 C.	6 C.
Green onion, chopped	2 T.	¼ C.	1/3 C.	½ C.	2/3 C.	¾ C.
Pecans, chopped	¼ C.	½ C.	¾ C.	1 C.	1¼ C.	1½ C.

Assembly Directions: Puree the sour cream, cream cheese, garlic powder, turkey breast and green onions in a food processor or blender. Stir in the chopped pecans.

Freezing Directions: Pour mixture into a labeled freezer bag or container. Remove the excess air, seal and freeze.

To Serve: Thaw mixture, stir well and pour into a small serving bowl. Serve with crackers, breads, or melba toast.

Comments: A 6-ounce can of diced chicken may replace the turkey. Reserve 1 C. of turkey from the day you roast and carve your holiday bird. This mixture makes a great filling for small party sandwiches. If you prefer a chunkier spread, use an electric mixer to mix up all the sour cream, cream cheese, garlic powder and Dijon mustard. Stir in the diced turkey, pecans and diced onions.

Lower Fat Options: Use low fat or fat free cream cheese, or Neufchatel. Use light or fat free sour cream to replace the full fat version. Omit the chopped nuts.

Storage Time: Refrigerator (40°): 3- 4 days, Freezer: 3 months

30 DAY GOURMET
APPETIZERS

Recipe: Cheese Wheel

Serves:	6	12	18	24	30	36
Quantity:	3 C.	6 C.	9 C.	12 C.	15 C.	18 C.
Ingredients:						
Mild cheddar cheese, shredded	8 oz.	16 oz.	24 oz.	32 oz.	40 oz.	48 oz.
Sharp cheddar cheese, shredded	8 oz.	16 oz.	24 oz.	32 oz.	40 oz.	48 oz.
Blue cheese, crumbled	2 oz.	4 oz.	6 oz.	8 oz.	10 oz.	12 oz.
Cream cheese, softened	16 oz.	32 oz.	48 oz.	64 oz.	80 oz.	96 oz.
Pecans, chopped	5 oz.	10 oz.	15 oz.	20 oz.	25 oz.	30 oz.

Assembly Directions: In a medium bowl, mix shredded cheeses and crumbled blue cheese. Mix in softened cream cheese with your hands or a sturdy wooden spoon until all the ingredients are evenly distributed. Spray coat or lightly grease an 8" round cake pan. Place a layer of plastic wrap in the pan so that it hangs over the edges all the way around. Fit it well into the bottom of the pan. The oil coating will help it stick and stay in place. Sprinkle ½ the chopped pecans in the bottom of the pan. Press the cheese mixture into the pan evenly, and smooth the top. Sprinkle on the remaining pecans and press them into the surface.

Freezing Directions: Set the unwrapped pan in the freezer and leave until firmly frozen (about an hour). Invert the pan onto a long sheet of plastic wrap (about 2 feet long). Remove the oiled plastic wrap and discard it. Use the excess plastic wrap under the cheese wheel to wrap the cheese wheel. Place the frozen wrapped cheese wheel inside a labeled freezer bag. Remove the excess air, seal and freeze.

To Serve: At least one hour before serving, remove the frozen cheese wheel from the bag and unwrap it. Place the cheese wheel on a flat plate or platter. Cover the cheese wheel loosely with the plastic. Set cheese wheel out at room temperature for one hour before serving.

Comments: The cheese mixture can be rolled in a ball, and then rolled in the chopped nuts for a traditional cheese ball. We feel that the flat version freezes and thaws faster and is easier to serve. For a spicier wheel, add ½ teaspoon garlic powder, ¼ teaspoon chili powder and a few drops of hot pepper sauce.

Lower Fat Options: Neufchatel, low fat, or fat free cream cheese may be used in place of the full fat cream cheese. Low or fat free shredded cheeses can be used in place of regular shredded cheeses. Crushed corn flakes or crisp rice cereal may be used to replace the chopped nuts.

Storage Time: Refrigerator (40°): 5-7 days, Freezer: 3 months

30 DAY GOURMET
MAIN DISHES/MEATS

Recipe: Roast Turkey and Gravy

Turkey, thawed	1 lb. per person
Butter, melted (optional)	
Celery ribs, cut in 4" long pieces	3 per turkey
Large onions, quartered	2 per turkey
Canned chicken broth	1 C. per lb.

Assembly Directions: Rinse the thawed turkey well, inside and out with cold water. Pat it dry with paper toweling. Place the turkey breast side up in the roasting pan. Place the celery and onion inside the body cavity. Rub or brush the turkey with the melted butter if you wish. Tear a sheet of foil 5 – 10 inches longer than the turkey. Make a crosswise crease through the center and place over the turkey. Crimp the foil loosely onto the edges of the pan. Roast according to the turkey roasting time chart. 20 to 30 minutes before the end of roasting, remove the foil. This will allow the turkey to brown. Use a meat thermometer and follow the manufacturer's instructions to be certain that the turkey is done. Leave the turkey in the pan to cool no more than two hours, then place it in its pan in the refrigerator to chill. When chilled, slice the meat lengthwise down the breast, and thighs. Bone the legs and any remaining meat.

Freezing Directions: Place the sliced meat into a labeled freezer bag or container. Pour the chicken broth over the meat. Seal and freeze.

To Serve: Thaw meat and broth in the bag or container. Bring to room temperature by allowing to sit out for up to, but not more than two hours. Place the meat and broth in an ovenproof pan. Cover with a lid or foil and heat at 350° for 30 minutes. The meat may be microwave reheated also. Place the meat and broth in a microwave safe container, cover with a lid or plastic wrap and heat on 50 % power for 12 – 15 minutes or until hot.

TURKEY GRAVY

Servings: ($\frac{1}{4}$ C. each)	6	12	18	24	30	36
Ingredients:						
Butter	1 T.	2 T.	3 T.	4 T.	5 T.	6 T.
Flour	3 T.	$\frac{1}{4}$ C. + 2 T.	$\frac{1}{2}$ C. + 1 T.	$\frac{3}{4}$ C.	$\frac{3}{4}$ C. + 3T.	1 C. + 2T.
Salt	$\frac{1}{4}$ t.	$\frac{1}{2}$ t.	$\frac{3}{4}$ t.	1 t.	$1\frac{1}{4}$ t.	$1\frac{1}{2}$ t.
Turkey broth, reserved and frozen	$1\frac{1}{2}$ C.	3 C.	$4\frac{1}{2}$ C.	6 C.	$7\frac{1}{2}$ C.	9 C.

Assembly Directions: Melt butter over low heat; mix in flour and salt. Heat and stir until bubbly. Add broth slowly, stirring constantly. Increase heat to medium high and stir constantly until gravy comes to a boil. Stir and boil one minute. Reduce heat to simmer and cook 2 – 3 minutes stirring occasionally.

Freezing Directions: To make your own turkey broth, place the cooked turkey bones and any remaining meat in a large pot. Crack the bones first if you can. Add enough water to cover the bones. Place a quartered onion, two or three ribs of celery and a carrot or two in the water for more flavor. Bring the pot to a boil. Reduce heat to simmer and cook for an hour. Watch carefully to not simmer pot dry, or boil over. Remove the bones and discard. Pour the broth through a strainer. Chill the broth. Remove any fat accumulated on top and discard it. Ladle or spoon the chilled broth into labeled freezer bags or containers in desired amounts. Seal and freeze.

To Serve: To use the broth, thaw completely, then bring to a boil before using.

NOTE: See page 2 for additional turkey information. USDA Turkey Hotline: 1-800-535-4555.

30 DAY GOURMET
MAIN DISHES/MEATS

Recipe: Rolled Beef Roast and Gravy

Servings:	6	12	18	24	30	36
Ingredients:						
Rolled rib roast	4 lbs.	8 lbs.	12 lbs.	16 lbs.	20 lbs.	24 lbs.
Beef Broth, canned	56 oz.	84 oz.	96 oz.	140 oz.	168 oz.	196 oz.
Beef bouillon granules	2 tsp.	1T. + 1t.	2 T.	2T. + 2t.	3T. + 1t.	4 T.
Milk	½ C.	1 C.	1½ C.	2 C.	2½ C.	3 C.
Cornstarch	¼ C.	½ C.	¾ C.	1 C.	1¼ C.	1½ C.

Assembly Directions for Meat: Place the meat (fatty side up) in a shallow roasting pan. Cover the meat with plastic wrap and allow it to sit at room temperature for about an hour and a half. Preheat the oven to 325°. Remove the plastic wrap and roast the meat uncovered for 20 minutes per pound, more or less. When a meat thermometer reads a temperature of 130°, the meat will be rare. At 140° it is medium, and well done at 160°. Because you will be reheating the meat, we suggest that you roast it to a temperature of just over 130°. This will help the meat to remain tender and not too well done after reheating. Allow the meat to cool completely. When the meat is cooled, cut the twine from the roast and discard it. Slice the roast across the grain into thin slices not more than ¼ inch thick.

Freezing Directions for Meat: Place the sliced meat into a labeled one-gallon freezer bag or suitable sized freezer container. Over the meat, pour enough canned beef broth to cover (about 1 C. per pound). Remove excess air from the bag, seal and freeze.

Assembly Directions for Gravy: For every 6 servings of roast, heat one cup of remaining canned beef broth to boiling, then pour it into the roasting pan the meat was cooked in. Use a fork to scrape up pan juices and caramelized drippings. Stir and break up any lumps. Pour drippings and broth into a 4-cup, glass measuring cup. Chill one hour, and then remove any fat that has risen to the top. Heat the drippings and broth in a microwave oven until it is boiling. Add the canned bouillon granules and stir until they have dissolved. Stir in the milk and enough additional broth to make 3 cups of liquid per 6 servings. Add the cornstarch to the broth and stir to dissolve.

Freezing Directions for Gravy: Pour all the gravy mixture into a labeled one-quart freezer bag. Seal and freeze the gravy.

To Serve Meat: Thaw meat container in refrigerator. Two hours before heating time, set the meat out at room temperature. 30 minutes before serving, place meat and broth into a baking pan or oven proof serving dish large enough to accommodate all of the contents. Cover the pan with foil or a lid and heat in a 350° oven for 30 minutes.

To Serve Gravy: Thaw gravy mixture. Set mixture out at room temperature two hours before heating time. Ten minutes before serving time, shake the bag vigorously and pour the gravy mixture into a saucepan. Stir and cook over medium high heat until it begins to boil. Reduce heat to a simmer and continue to cook for two minutes, stirring occasionally. Pour gravy into serving dish and serve with beef roast.

Storage Time: Refrigerator (40°): 3-4 days, Freezer: 2-3 months

Recipes: Holiday Pork Roast with Gravy

Servings:	6	12	18	24	30	36
Ingredients:						
Boneless pork loin roast	4 lb.	8 lb.	12 lb.	16 lb.	20 lb.	24 lb.
Chicken broth	56 oz.	84 oz.	96 oz.	140 oz.	168 oz.	196 oz.

Gravy:						
Beef bouillon granules	2 t.	1T. + 1t.	2 T.	2T. + 2t.	3T. + 1t.	4 T.
Worcestershire sauce	½ t.	1 t.	1½ t.	2 t.	2½ t.	1 T.
Milk	½ C.	1 C.	1½ C.	2 C.	2½ C.	3 C.
Cornstarch	¼ C.	½ C.	¾ C.	1 C.	1¼ C.	1½ C.
Water	¼ C.	½ C.	¾ C.	1 C.	1¼ C.	1½ C.

Assembly Directions for Meat: Place pork roast in an ungreased shallow roasting pan or baking dish. Cook meat in a 350° oven for one hour. Continue roasting until a meat thermometer reads 155°. Remove the pan of meat from the oven and allow to cool to room temperature, then chill thoroughly. When meat is chilled, place it on a cutting board and slice it crosswise into ¼ inch slices.

Freezing Directions for Meat: Place the sliced meat into a labeled 1-gallon freezer bag. Cover the meat with chicken broth. Remove excess air from the bag, seal and freeze.

Assembly Directions for Gravy: For every 6 servings of roast, pour one cup of broth, heated to boiling into the roasting pan. Use a fork to scrape up all the drippings and caramelized meat juices. Stir and break up any lumps. Pour the broth and drippings into a small bowl and place into refrigerator for at least one hour. When the broth has cooled, the fat will have risen to the top. Remove the fat with a spoon and discard. In the microwave or in a sauce pan on the stove, heat the broth until it just reaches the boiling point. Stir in the bouillon granules until they dissolve. Stir in the milk, then add chicken broth to make 3 C. of liquid per 6 servings. Add the cornstarch and stir to dissolve.

Freezing Directions for Gravy: Pour all the gravy mixture into a labeled one-quart freezer bag. Remove excess air from the bag, seal and freeze.

To Serve Meat: Thaw meat in the broth. Set meat and broth out at room temperature two hours before heating time. 30 minutes before serving, place the meat and broth into a baking pan or oven-proof serving dish large enough to accommodate all the contents. Cover the pan with foil and place in a 350° oven for 30 minutes.

To Serve Gravy: Thaw the gravy bag. Set the gravy mixture out at room temperature two hours before heating time. Ten minutes before serving time shake sealed gravy container vigorously and pour the entire contents into a saucepan large enough to accommodate all of it. Over medium high heat, continuously stir pan until it comes to a boil and begins to thicken. Reduce heat to a simmer and continue to simmer and stir occasionally for two or three minutes. Pour gravy into serving dish.

Storage Time: Refrigerator (40°): 3-4 days, Freezer: 2-3 months

Recipe: Old Fashioned Bread Dressing

Serves:	6	12	18	24	30	36
Ingredients:						
Butter/Margarine	2 T.	4 T.	6 T.	8 T.	10 T.	12 T.
Onion, diced (1 med = 1 C.)	1 C.	2 C.	3 C.	4 C.	5 C.	6 C.
Celery, diced (1 med rib = 1½ C.)	1 C.	2 C.	3 C.	4 C.	5 C.	6 C.
Ground black pepper	¼ t.	½ t.	¾ t.	1 t.	1¼ t.	1½ t.
Salt	½ t.	1 t.	1½ t.	2 t.	2½ t.	1 T.
Poultry seasoning	½ t.	1 t.	1½ t.	2 t.	2½ t.	1 T.
Bread (20 oz. loaf) Or	1	2	3	4	5	6
Purchased dried stuffing bread/cornbread Or	14 oz.	28 oz.	42 oz.	56 oz.	70 oz.	84 oz.
Stale Cornbread	6 C.	12 C.	18 C.	24 C.	30 C.	36 C.
Chicken broth, canned	14.5 oz.	29 oz.	43.5 oz.	58 oz.	72.5 oz.	87 oz.
Options:						
Raisins	1 C.	2 C.	3 C.	4 C.	5 C.	6 C.
Walnuts or pecans, chopped	½ C.	1 C.	1½ C.	2 C.	2½ C.	3 C.
Fresh mushrooms, sliced	1 C.	2 C.	3 C.	4 C.	5 C.	6 C.
Bacon, cooked and crumbled	½ C.	1 C.	1½ C.	2 C.	2½ C.	3 C.
Tart unpeeled apples, diced	1 C.	2 C.	3 C.	4 C.	5 C.	6 C.

Assembly Directions: If starting with fresh bread, cut it into ½ inch or one inch cubes. Place each 6 serving recipe in two 9x13 pans or one larger roasting pan. Toast the bread cubes in the oven at 300° for one hour, stirring occasionally, then remove pan from oven and cool bread cubes. Melt the butter in a skillet. Sauté the onions and celery over medium heat until they just start to become transparent. Sprinkle pepper, salt, and poultry seasoning over onions and celery. Continue cooking two or three minutes. Add any of the optional ingredients now and continue cooking for 5 minutes. Remove from heat. Stir in chicken broth. Pour all pan ingredients over bread in a large bowl. Stir to coat bread well and allow to cool completely.

Freezing Directions: When cool, place the dressing mixture into a labeled one-gallon bag(s). Remove excess air from bag, seal and freeze.

To Serve: Thaw dressing mixture completely. Two hours before heating time, set dressing out at room temperature. 30 minutes before serving time, place entire dressing mixture into an oiled ovenproof baking pan or serving container. Bake uncovered at 350° for 30 minutes. Remove from heat and serve.

Lower Fat Alternatives: Steam the vegetables in a saucepan or the microwave instead of sautéing them in butter. Stir the seasonings into the steamed vegetables. Use fat free chicken broth. For optional ingredients choose apples, mushrooms or raisins instead of the bacon and nuts.

Storage Time: Baked: Refrigerator (40°): 4-6 days, Freezer: 2-3 months
Unbaked: Refrigerator (40°): 2-4 days, Freezer: 2-3 months

Recipe: **Classic Cranberry Relish**

Serves:	6	12	18	24	30	36
Ingredients:						
Canned whole cranberry sauce	16 oz.	32 oz.	48 oz.	64 oz.	80 oz.	96 oz.
Brown sugar, to taste	2-3 T.	4-6 T.	6-9 T.	8-12 T.	10-15 T.	12-18 T.
Orange peel, grated *	2 t.	1T.+1t.	2 T.	2T. + 2t.	3T. + 1t.	4 T.

Assembly Directions: Combine all ingredients well. Place in a labeled one-quart freezer bag. Remove excess air from bag, seal and freeze.

To serve: Thaw the bag of sauce. Place sauce in a small microwave safe dish and cover with plastic wrap. Microwave on 100% power one minute or until hot.

Comments: This sauce is wonderful served with the pork roast, or turkey.

Storage Time: Refrigerator (40°): 4-6 days, Freezer: 2-3 months

*How to GRATE ORANGE PEEL - There are specially made orange zesters on the market that do a great job, but if you don't happen to have one handy, use a small sharp knife to peel off just the bright orange portion of the orange peel. The white part is bitter. Using a larger chopping knife, mince the peel very fine, or into very thin strips.

Recipe: Sweet Potato Soufflé with Brown Sugar Crumbles

Servings:	6	12	18	24	30	36
Ingredients:						
Sweet potatoes, canned Or	40 oz.	80 oz.	120 oz.	160 oz.	200 oz.	240 oz.
Sweet potatoes, freshly cooked	2 ½ lbs.	5 lbs.	7½ lbs.	10 lbs.	12½ lbs.	15 lbs.
Milk	¼ C.	½ C.	¾ C.	1 C.	1¼ C.	1½ C.
Butter/margarine, melted and cooled	½ C.	1 C.	1½ C.	2 C.	2½ C.	3 C.
Sugar	3/4 C.	1½ C.	2¼ C.	3 C.	3¾ C.	4½ C.
Eggs	2	4	6	8	10	12
Vanilla extract	1 T.	2 T.	3 T.	¼ C.	¼C. + 1T.	¼C, + 2T.
Brown sugar	1 C.	2 C.	3 C.	4 C.	5 C.	6 C.
Flour	½ C.	1 C.	1½ C.	2 C.	2½ C.	3 C.
Butter/margarine, chilled	1/3 C.	2/3 C.	1 C.	1 1/3 C.	1 2/3 C.	2 C.
Walnuts or pecans, chopped	1 C.	2 C.	3 C.	4 C.	5 C.	6 C.

Assembly Directions: With a potato masher, electric mixer, or food processor, puree the sweet potatoes. You will end up with about 3 cups of puree per 6 servings. With a whisk or electric mixer, add milk, melted butter, sugar, eggs and vanilla extract. In another bowl, stir together the brown sugar and flour. Slice the chilled butter into the brown sugar mixture. With your fingers, a fork or pastry blender, blend in the butter until the mixture is crumbly and evenly mixed. Stir in the chopped nuts.

Freezing Directions: Place the sweet potato mixture in a labeled one-gallon freezer bag(s) or container. Remove the excess air from the container, seal and freeze. Place the brown sugar crumbles in a labeled quart size freezer bag(s).   Remove excess air, seal and freeze.

To Serve: Thaw both bags. Spread sweet potato mixture in a greased or spray coated baking dish. Evenly distribute the crumbles over the sweet potatoes. Bake at 350° for 25 – 30 minutes.

Comments: To cook fresh sweet potatoes, scrub and peel them, place them in a pan and cover with water. Bring to a boil, reduce heat to a simmer and cook until they can be easily pierced with a fork. Drain well. For a richer version, use evaporated skim milk or cream to replace the milk.

Lower Fat Options: Use skim milk and cut the butter in the sweet potato mixture in half. Replace each whole egg with two egg whites. The nuts may be omitted, but it won't be the same!

Storage Time:
Baked: Refrigerator (40°): 4-6 days, Freezer: 2-3 months
Unbaked :   Refrigerator (40°): 2-4 days, Freezer: 2-3 months

Recipe: Carrots with Cashew Butter

Servings:	6	12	18	24	30	36
Ingredients:						
Fresh baby carrots	2 lbs.	4 lbs.	6 lbs.	8 lbs.	10 lbs.	12 lbs.
Chicken broth, canned	2 C.	4 C.	6 C.	8 C.	10 C.	12 C.
Cashews, roasted, salted	4 oz.	8 oz.	12 oz.	16 oz.	20 oz.	24 oz.
Butter/Margarine, softened	½ C.	1 C.	1½ C.	2 C.	2½ C.	3 C.
Honey	2 t.	1T. + 1 t.	2 T.	2T. + 2t.	3T. + 1 t.	4 T.
Or Sugar	1 T.	2 T.	3 T.	¼ C.	¼ C. + 1T.	½ C. + 2 T.

Assembly Directions: In a saucepan bring the chicken broth to a rolling boil. Carefully place the baby carrots into the broth. Return broth to a boil and cook 3 minutes. Remove from heat and allow to cool completely. While carrots are cooling, chop the cashews into pea size pieces. In a small bowl, stir together the softened butter/margarine, honey or sugar, and chopped nuts.

Freezing Directions: Place the butter/margarine mixture into a labeled pint size freezer bag(s) or container. Remove excess air from the bag, seal and freeze. When the carrots and broth have reached room temperature, pour them into a labeled one-gallon freezer bag(s). Remove excess air from bag, seal and freeze in a thin flat layer. Keep the two freezer bags together by placing both into a large freezer or food storage bag.

To Serve: Thaw container of carrots and cashew butter. Pour mixture into a saucepan. Bring to a boil, then reduce heat to a simmer and cook 10 minutes or until carrots are tender. Salt and pepper to taste, then place carrots and remaining broth in a serving dish. Place the cashew butter in the hot saucepan. When it has melted, pour it over the carrots. Serve immediately.

Comments: The cashew butter is optional.

Lower Fat Options: The cashew butter may be omitted, or the amount of butter cut in half.

Storage Time: Refrigerator (40°): 7 days, Freezer: 2-3 months

30 DAY GOURMET
VEGETABLES

Recipe: Veggie Medley

Serves:	6	12	18	24	30	36
Ingredients:						
Canned cream of chicken soup, undiluted (10.5 oz.)	2 cans (21 oz.)	4 cans (42 oz.)	6 cans (63 oz.)	8 cans (84 oz.)	10 cans (105 oz.)	12 cans (126 oz.)
Onion, diced (1 med = 1 C.)	½ C.	1 C.	1½ C.	2 C.	2½ C.	3 C.
Celery, diced (1 med rib = 1½ C.)	½ C.	1 C.	1½ C.	2 C.	2½ C.	3 C.
Frozen mixed vegetables	16 oz.	32 oz.	48 oz.	64 oz.	80 oz.	96 oz.
Seasoned croutons Or	6 oz.	12 oz.	18 oz.	24 oz.	30 oz.	36 oz.
Toasted bread cubes *	3 C.	6 C.	9 C.	12 C.	15 C.	18 C.
Cheddar or American cheese, shredded	2 C. (8 oz.)	4 C. (16 oz.)	6 C. (24 oz.)	8 C. (32 oz.)	10 C. (40 oz.)	12 C. (48 oz.)

Assembly Directions: Combine soup with the onion and celery. If the vegetables are frozen in clumps, break them apart. In a large bowl, toss the frozen vegetables with the croutons or bread cubes. Stir the sauce mixture into the vegetable mixture.

Freezing Directions: Place the entire mixture into a labeled one-gallon freezer bag(s). Remove the excess air, seal and freeze.

To Serve: Thaw bag thoroughly and bring to room temperature for two hours. Place mixture into an oiled baking dish. Top with shredded cheese. Bake at 350° for 30 minutes until vegetables are soft and cheese is melted.

This could also be cooked in the microwave, but the croutons will not be crunchy on top. Cook in a covered microwave safe container without the cheese at 100% power for 10 minutes. Stir once, then top with cheese. Cover and continue cooking at 100 % power for 5-7 more minutes until the vegetables are fork tender and the cheese is melted and bubbly.

Comments: Any mixture of frozen vegetables is fine.

Lower Fat Options: *Freezer Cooking Manual* owners may use 3 C. of the Fat-free White Sauce recipe as a substitute for every 2 cans of soup. You may, of course, purchase fat free or low fat canned soups. The cheese topping may be omitted or substitute low fat or fat free cheese. Read crouton package labels. Some are baked without added fat, some are fried. Toasted bread cubes are a good option. To toast bread cubes, cut bread slices into ½" to 1" cubes. Place in a single layer in an ungreased rimmed baking pan and bake at 300° for 10 minutes. Turn the cubes with a spatula, then continue baking until browned. Cool in the pan.

Freezer Storage Time: Baked: Refrigerator (40°): 4-6 days, Freezer: 2-3 months
Unbaked: Refrigerator (40°): 2-4 days, Freezer: 2-3 months

* If you use the bread cubes, you can add seasonings to the sauce if you wish. Add ¼ teaspoon of garlic powder, ¼ teaspoon of oregano, and ¼ teaspoon of parsley flakes.

Recipe: Duchess Mashed Potatoes

Servings:	6	12	18	24	30	36
	12 rosettes	24 rosettes	36 rosettes	48 rosettes	60 rosettes	72 rosettes
Ingredients:						
Russet potatoes, peeled and quartered	1 1/2 lbs. (5 med.)	3 lbs. (10 med.)	5½ lbs. (15 med.)	7 lbs. (20 med.)	8½ lbs. (25 med.)	10 lbs. (30 med.)
Butter/margarine	3 T.	6 T.	9 T.	12 T.	15 T.	18 T.
Eggs, beaten	2	4	6	8	10	12
Salt	½ t.	1 t.	1½ t.	2 t.	2½ t.	1 T.
Paprika (optional)						

Assembly Directions: Place the potatoes in a large pan. Add enough water to cover the potatoes. Place them on the stove over high heat and bring the water to a boil. Reduce the heat to simmer. Cook the potatoes until just fork tender (about 15 minutes). Remove from heat and drain well (about 5 minutes drain time). In a large mixing bowl, mash the potatoes by hand or with mixer until no lumps remain. Return the potatoes to the pan and stir over medium low heat for three minutes, being careful not to let them brown (this is to evaporate some of the moisture from the potatoes). Remove from heat and mix in butter. Cool 10 minutes in the pan, then mix in beaten eggs and salt.

For Rosette Puffs: For fancy rosette shaped potato puffs, attach a large rosette-piping tip to a piping bag. Oil a large baking sheet. Place the cooled potato mixture in the piping bag and pipe into 12 spiral shaped rosettes per 6 servings. This will take about 1/3 cup of potato mixture for each rosette. Spray the rosettes lightly with spray oil and dust with paprika. Bake in a 400° oven 15 minutes or so until lightly browned.

Freezing Directions for plain Mashed Potatoes: Freeze the cooled potato mixture in a thin layer in a labeled one-gallon freezer bag(s).

Freezing Directions for Rosette Puffs: Allow to cool on the baking sheet, then place the pan and potatoes in the freezer, uncovered. Freeze until potatoes are solid. Remove the frozen potatoes from the sheet and place in a labeled one-gallon freezer bag. Remove excess air, seal and freeze.

To Serve:

Casserole: Place thawed potato mixture in an oiled ovenproof dish. Smooth or swirl the top, spray lightly with spray cooking oil and dust with paprika. Bake at 350° for 30 minutes or microwave heat at 50% power for 15 minutes or until hot throughout.

Rosette Puffs: Place frozen rosettes on an oiled baking sheet. Thaw them on the sheet. Reheat at 350° for 20 minutes or until hot. These are beautiful arranged around sliced roasted meats.

Comments: To save on clean up, line the pans with aluminum foil, then oil the foil and place the potatoes on them. If you like, you may use butter flavored spray oil. You might want to plan to make extra potatoes to use as an ingredient in the Easy No-Knead Potato Rolls.

Lower Fat Options: Use 2 egg whites to replace each egg.

Storage Time:
Baked: Refrigerator (40°): 4-6 days, Freezer: 2-3 months
Unbaked: Refrigerator (40°): 2-4 days, Freezer: 2-3 months

30 DAY GOURMET
BREADS

Recipe: Easy No Knead Potato Rolls

Quantity:	45 rolls	90 rolls	135 rolls	180 rolls	225 rolls	270 rolls
Ingredients:						
Sugar	2/3 C.	1 1/3 C.	2 C.	2 2/3 C.	3 1/3 C.	4 C.
Shortening	2/3 C.	1 1/3 C.	2 C.	2 2/3 C.	3 1/3 C.	4 C.
Unseasoned mashed potatoes	1 C.	2 C.	3 C.	4 C.	5 C.	6 C.
Salt	2 ½ t.	1T. + 2t.	2T. + 1½ t.	3T. + 1 t.	¼ C. + ½ t.	¼ C. + 1T.
Eggs	2	4	6	8	10	12
Active dry yeast pkts.	2	4	6	8	10	12
Warm water, divided	1 1/3 C.	2 2/3 C.	4 C.	5 1/3 C.	6 2/3 C.	8 C.
All purpose flour	6-6 ½ C.	12-13 C.	18-19½ C.	24-26 C.	30-32½ C.	36-39 C.

Assembly Directions: In a small bowl, dissolve the yeast in half of the warm water. In a large mixing bowl, combine sugar, shortening, and potatoes, and salt. Add the eggs. Mix in the dissolved yeast mixture. Mix in half of the flour and the remaining water. With a dough hook or a wooden spoon, mix in as much of the remaining flour as possible to form a soft dough. Place the dough in a greased bowl that is twice the size of the dough. Turn the dough over in the bowl once to grease all sides. Cover the bowl with a lid or plastic wrap. Set the bowl in a warm, draft free environment and allow to rise until the dough has doubled in size. It will take about an hour. Punch your fist into the middle of the raised dough to deflate it. Divide the dough into thirds. Shape each third into 15 balls. Grease three 8 or 9" round cake or pie pans. Place 15 dough balls in each pan. Cover the pans loosely with plastic wrap and let rise again until doubled (about 30 minutes). Bake at 325° until just beginning to turn brown (about 15 minutes). Remove from the oven and use a spatula or fork to pull the rolls apart and cool on racks. Do not cut the rolls apart, it will mash the edges.

Freezing Directions: When the rolls are cool, place them on a cookie pan and freeze unwrapped until firm. Place frozen rolls into a labeled freezer bag or container. Remove excess air, seal and freeze.

To Serve: Thaw rolls in the bag for 10 – 15 minutes. Place rolls on ungreased baking sheet. Heat oven to 400°. Place rolls on top rack of oven and bake about 10 minutes until browned.

Comments: Prepare each batch separately. Use the multiplied equivalents to make your shopping lists, but your mixer bowl will not accommodate doubling the recipe. These rolls are very small, you can eat several before feeling the effects! ☺

Recipe: Easy Brown and Serve Rolls from Purchased Frozen Dough

Quantity:		24	48	72	96	120	144
Ingredients:							
Frozen roll dough, 25 oz. bag		1	2	3	4	5	6

Assembly Directions: Grease two 8 or 9 inch cake or pie pans. Place 12 frozen dough balls in each pan. Cover loosely with plastic wrap and allow to sit in a warm, draft free environment until they have doubled in size, about 2 ½ hours. Bake in a preheated 325° oven for about 10 – 15 minutes until just turning brown. Slide rolls out of the pan onto a cooling rack. Cool completely.

Freezing Directions: Place cooling racks of rolls into freezer and freeze until firm. When firm, place frozen rolls in a labeled freezer bag. Remove excess air, seal and freeze.

To Serve: Thaw the rolls in their packaging for 10 – 15 minutes. Place rolls back into the pan (ungreased) they were pre-baked in. Preheat oven to 400°. Place the rolls on the top rack of the oven and bake about 10 minutes, until well browned.

Storage Time: Raw dough: Refrigerator (40°): 6-8 hours, Freezer: 2 weeks
                  Brown and Serve: Refrigerator (40°): 2-3 days, Freezer: 12 months
                  Fully Baked: Refrigerator (40°): 2-3 days, Freezer: 12-15 months

Recipe: Celebration Salad

Servings:	6	12	18	24	30	36
Ingredients:						
Orange rind, grated	2 t.	1T. + 1 t.	2 T.	2T. + 2t.	3T. + 1 t.	¼ C.
Crushed pineapple, drained	8 ounce	16 oz.	24 oz.	32 oz.	40 oz.	48 oz.
Lemon juice	2 T.	¼ C.	1/3 C.	½ C.	2/3 C.	¾ C.
Canned WHOLE cranberry sauce	16 oz.	32 oz.	48 oz.	64 oz.	80 oz.	96 oz.
Whipped topping	2 C. (8 oz.)	4 C. (16 oz.)	6 C. (24 oz.)	8 C. (32 oz.)	10 C. (40 oz.)	12 C. (48 oz.)
Walnuts or pecans, chopped	¾ cup	1½ C.	2¼ C.	3 C.	3¾ C.	4½ C.
Celery, finely diced	¼ cup	½ C.	¾ C.	1 C.	1¼ C.	1½ C.
Candied fruits for garnish (optional)						

Assembly Directions: Combine orange rind, pineapple, lemon juice, and cranberry sauce. Pour into an oiled 6-cup mold, serving container, or shallow freezer container. Serving container or freezer container does not need to be oiled. To oil a salad mold, spray lightly with cooking spray, or oil your hands with shortening or cooking oil and rub all over the inside surface if the mold. Spread the cranberry mixture evenly with a spoon or spatula. Combine whipped topping, nuts and celery. Spread over the cranberry mixture. When freezing in a mold, the white layer will be on the bottom. Serving from a container will put the white layer on top.

Freezing Directions: Cover the salad with the container lid, plastic wrap, or slide it inside a 2-gallon freezer bag. Freeze on a level surface so the salad does not become lopsided.

To Serve: Set the salad out at room temperature about 10 minutes before serving. Molded salads should be inverted onto chilled serving plates.   If the salad does not come out of the mold easily, dip the mold in hot water for about ten seconds and then unmold. Salad frozen in serving container or freezer container can be sliced into squares and served onto chilled plates.

Comments: The candied fruits may be used to decorate the surface of the salad that is served from a container. A pretty design can be made with them on the white layer before freezing, or the salad can be cut and then decorated after it is on serving plates.

Lower Fat Alternatives: Use low fat or fat free whipped topping. Reduce the amount of chopped nuts or omit them completely.

Storage Time: Keep frozen (do not refrigerate), Freezer: 2-3 months

Recipe: Frozen Waldorf Salad

Servings:	6	12	18	24	30	36
Ingredients:						
Apples	2	4	6	8	10	12
Lemon juice	¼ C.	½ C.	¾ C.	1 C.	1¼ C	1½ C.
Crushed pineapple, drained with juice reserved	½ C.	1 C.	1½ C.	2 C.	2½ C.	3 C.
Eggs	2	4	6	8	10	12
Sugar	½ C.	1 C.	1½ C.	2 C.	2½ C.	3 C.
Salt	1/8 t.	¼ t.	¼ t. + 1/8 t.	½ t.	½ t. + 1/8 t.	¾ t.
Celery, diced (1 med. rib=1½ C.)	½ C.	1 C.	1½ C.	2 C.	2½ C.	3 C.
Walnuts, coarsely chopped	½ C.	1 C.	1½ C.	2 C.	2½ C.	3 C.
Seedless grapes, halved (optional)	1 C.	2 C.	3 C.	4 C.	5 C.	6 C.
Whipped topping	2 C. (16 oz.)	4 C. (32 oz.)	6 C. (48 oz.)	8 C. (64 oz.)	10 C. (80 oz.)	12 C. (96 oz.)

Assembly Directions: Core and dice unpeeled apples. In a small bowl, pour the lemon juice over the apple pieces and toss to coat well with a fork or spoon. Place a strainer over the bowl and drain the crushed pineapple in it so that the juice pours over the apples. Use the spoon or fork to press the juice out of the pineapple until it is fairly dry. Place the drained pineapple aside in a small container. Set the strainer over a microwaveable bowl. Pour the apples and juice through the strainer. Place the drained apples into the container with the pineapple, and set it aside. To the bowl of juices, add the eggs, sugar and salt. Mix well with the fork or spoon. Place the bowl of egg mixture into the microwave and cook on 100 % power for one minute, then stir well. Repeat cooking for one minute and stirring until the mixture has formed a thin custard that will coat the spoon or fork and resemble melted ice cream. The procedure may need to be repeated four or five times depending on the microwave. Cover the bowl with plastic wrap or a pie plate and cool to room temperature. When cooled, add celery, nuts, and fruits, stirring well. With a rubber spatula or wooden spoon, fold in whipped topping.

Freezing Directions:
Option 1: Divide the mixture evenly between custard cups, oiled individual molds, or one oiled larger (6-8 cup) mold. Cover the mold with plastic wrap or foil and freeze. To oil the molds, spray lightly with spray pan coating, or oil your hands with shortening or vegetable oil and rub all over the inside of the mold.
Option 2: Spread the salad mixture evenly into a shallow freezer container or serving dish. Cover with plastic wrap. Place wrapped dish inside a one or two-gallon freezer bag, seal and freeze.
To Serve: Set frozen salads out about 10 minutes before serving time. If molded salads do not come out easily, dip mold in hot water for about ten seconds and then unmold onto a cold plate. Salads frozen in a shallow freezer container or serving dish may be cut into squares and served from the container with a spatula. The salads look very pretty on a dark green lettuce leaf on a chilled plate.
Comments: Vary the colors of the ingredients to fit the occasion. For Christmas, use darker green and red apples, seedless red or green grapes. For Thanksgiving, choose the softer colored fruits. For Easter, choose pale yellow and green apples. For Independence Day, choose dark red apples, and seedless blue grapes.
Lower Fat Alternatives: Replace the whipped topping with lower fat or fat free whipped topping.
Storage Time: Keep frozen (do not refrigerate), Freezer: 2-3 months

Recipe: Layered Pumpkin Cheesecake

Servings:	1 Pie	2 Pies	3 Pies	4 Pies	5 Pies	6 Pies
Ingredients:						
Cream cheese, softened	24 oz.	48 oz.	72 oz.	96 oz.	120 oz.	144 oz.
Sugar	¾ C.	1½ C.	2¼ C.	3 C.	3¾ C.	4½ c.
Vanilla	1 t.	2 t.	1 T.	1T. + 1t.	1T. + 2t	2 T.
Eggs	3	6	9	12	15	18
Canned pumpkin	¾ C. (6 oz.)	1½ C. (12 oz.)	2¼ C. (18 oz.)	3 C. (24 oz.)	3¾ C. (32 oz.)	4½ C. (40 oz.)
Cinnamon	½ t.	1 t.	1½ t.	2 t.	2½ t.	1 T.
Cloves	1/8 t.	¼ t.	3/8 t.	½ t.	½t.+1/8t.	¾ t.
Graham cracker crust, 9 ounce (extra large)	1	2	3	4	5	6

Assembly Directions: Assemble each pie separately. Mix cream cheese, sugar, and vanilla at low speed of electric mixer until well blended. Add eggs one at a time, mixing well after each one. Set aside 1½ cups of cheesecake mixture in a separate bowl. Pour remaining cheesecake mixture into graham cracker crust and smooth with a spatula or spoon. Stir the pumpkin into the remaining 1½ cups of cheesecake mixture. Sprinkle spices over the pumpkin cheesecake mixture and then blend in well. Spoon the pumpkin cheesecake mixture over the cheesecake mixture in the graham cracker crust. Bake in a 350° preheated oven for 40 minutes, then turn off oven and let cheesecake set until the oven is completely cooled.

Freezing Directions: Cool cheesecake to room temperature then set on a shelf in the freezer and freeze until firm. Cover the cheesecake with a layer of plastic wrap. Place frozen cheesecake inside a labeled 2-gallon freezer bag. Remove excess air, seal and return to freezer.

To Serve: Remove cheesecake from bag. Loosen plastic wrap and leave loosely covered at room temperature for two hours before serving.

Lower Fat Alternatives: Substitute the cream cheese with lower fat cream cheese or Neufchatel. Use 2 egg whites to replace each egg.

Storage Time: Refrigerator (40°): 4-6 days, Freezer: 2-3 months

Recipe: Merry Kiss-Mousse Pie

Servings:	1 Pie	2 pies	3 pies	4 pies	5 pies	6 pies
Ingredients:						
Semi sweet chocolate chips	12 oz.	24 oz.	36 oz.	48 oz.	60 oz.	72 oz.
Whipping cream, divided	16 oz.	32 oz.	48 oz.	64 oz.	80 oz.	96 oz.
Powdered sugar	¼ C.	½ C.	¾ C.	1 C.	1¼ C.	1½ C.
Vanilla extract	2 t.	1T. + 1t.	2 T.	2T. + 2t.	3T. + 1t.	¼ C.
9 inch chocolate crumb crust	1	2	3	4	5	6
Whipped topping	2 C.	4 C.	6 C.	8 C.	10 C.	12 C.
Chocolate kiss shaped candy	15 candies	30 candies	45 candies	60 candies	75 candies	90 candies

Assembly Directions: Assemble each pie individually. In a microwave safe bowl, combine the chocolate chips and ½ cup of the whipping cream. Cook on 100% power for one minute, then stir. Cook 30 seconds and stir. Continue to cook and stir until the mixture can be stirred smooth. Set bowl in a pan or sink of cold water to cool. Stir occasionally to speed cooling. Mix the powdered sugar and vanilla extract with the melted chocolate chips. Meanwhile, fill the bottom of the cookie crust with unwrapped kiss candies to cover the bottom, pointed end up. In a medium mixing bowl, pour in remaining 1½ cup whipping cream. Beat on high just until soft peaks begin to form. Spoon in about ¼ cup of the cooled melted chocolate mixture and mix well. Continue adding chocolate mixture ¼ cup at a time until it is all incorporated (do not beat too long or you will make chocolate flavored butter!) When the chocolate is all mixed in, spoon the mixture into the crust carefully to not disturb the chocolate candies.

Freezing: Smooth the top of the pie and refrigerate several hours before serving, or set into freezer until firm. Place the frozen pie into a large labeled freezer bag, or wrap well with heavy plastic wrap.

To Serve: Set out at room temperature at least one hour before serving or thaw in refrigerator. Just before serving, top with 2 cups of whipped topping and decorate with additional candies.

Comments: Peppermint patty candies may be substituted for kiss candies.

Lower Fat Alternatives: Use low fat or fat free whipped topping for garnishing. Replace the chocolate candies with a lower fat or fat free candy of your choice or omit completely.

Storage Time: Refrigerator (40°): 4-6 days, Freezer: 2-3 months

30 DAY GOURMET
DESSERTS

Recipe: Frosty Pumpkin-Vanilla Pie

Servings:	1 Pie	2 Pies	3 Pies	4 Pies	5 Pies	6 Pies
Ingredients:						
9 oz. graham cracker pie crust	1	2	3	4	5	6
Vanilla flavored frozen yogurt, slightly softened	2 C.	4 C.	6 C.	8 C.	10 C.	12 C.
Canned pumpkin	15oz.	30 oz.	45 oz.	60 oz.	75 oz.	90 oz.
Sugar	¾ C.	1½ C.	2¼ C.	3 C.	3¾ C.	4½ C.
Cinnamon	1 t.	2 t.	1 T.	1T + 1t.	1T + 2 t.	2 T.
Ginger	½ t.	1 t.	1½ t.	2 t.	2½ t.	3 t.
Imitation rum flavoring (opt.)	2 t.	1T. + 1 t.	2 T.	2T. + 2t.	3T. + 1t.	4 T.
Whipped topping	16 oz.	32 oz.	48 oz.	64 oz.	80 oz.	96 oz.
Or						
Whipped cream *	2 C.	4 C.	6 C.	8 C.	10 C.	12 C.

Assembly Directions: Spread slightly softened frozen yogurt into pie shell. Smooth with a spoon then place in the freezer. Freeze until firm. When the yogurt layer is firmly frozen, stir together the pumpkin, sugar, spices and rum flavoring. Fold in the whipped topping. Spoon this mixture over the frozen yogurt layer. Return the pie to the freezer and freeze until firm.

Freezing Directions: When firm, cover the pie with plastic wrap and place inside a labeled 2-gallon freezer bag. Remove excess air, seal bag and return to freezer.

To Serve: Set frozen pie out at room temperature for 10 minutes. Slice, and serve frozen with extra whipped cream or whipped topping to garnish.

Lower Fat Alternatives: Use fat free or low fat frozen yogurt to replace the regular frozen yogurt. Use lower fat or fat free whipped topping to replace the whipped cream.

***How to WHIP CREAM** – Nanci wouldn't dream of "whipping her own" but Tara believes that the real thing far outshines the frozen version sold in a white tub. It helps to have immaculately clean beaters, bowl, and rubber spatula for this job. Buy heavy or whipping cream, they are the same thing. Make sure the cream is well chilled. Place the bowl and beaters in the freezer at least 5 or 10 minutes before whipping. Pour the chilled cream into the chilled bowl. Beat with an electric mixer on high, scraping with a spatula once or twice if needed, until the cream forms soft peaks. Watch it carefully – if you beat it too long it will begin to turn to butter. Whipping cream will double in volume after it has been whipped. One cup of whipping cream will yield two cups of whipped cream. One to two Tablespoons of powdered sugar and ½ teaspoon of vanilla extract or other flavoring may be added any time to each cup of heavy cream during whipping.

FOR LOW FAT WHIPPED CREAM: Substitute chilled canned evaporated skim milk. It will whip very nicely. This may be substituted for whipping cream in any of the recipes in this book.

Storage Time: Keep frozen (do not refrigerate), Freezer: 2-3 months

Recipe: Easy Pie Crusts

Many fruit pie fillings freeze very well. Included in this book are some traditional favorites. These can be used in double crust pies, or single crust pies with a crumb topping. These pie fillings will fill an eight or nine inch deep dish pie shell. Some people would never dream of purchasing a frozen pie crust, while others would never dream of making one "from scratch". We suggest that you use whichever option you are most comfortable with. Below we have given you a single and double pie crust recipe, and a crumb topping to be used with a single deep dish crust pie (purchased, or homemade).

9" single pie shell

Servings	1 pie	2 pies	3 pies	4 pies	5 pies	6 pies
Ingredients:						
Flour	1½ C.	3 C.	4½ C.	6 C.	7½ C.	9 C.
Salt	¼ t.	½ t.	¾ t.	1 t.	1¼ t.	1½ t.
Shortening	½ C.	1 C.	1½ C.	2 C.	2½ C.	3 C.
Ice water	3-4 T.	6-8 T.	9-12 T.	12-16 T.	15-20 T.	18-24 T.

Mix flour and salt. Cut the shortening into the flour with a pastry blender or two knives until it resembles crumbs that are the size of split peas or grains of rice. The crumbs will not be uniform in size and that is o.k. Sprinkle the water over the flour a little at a time and toss LIGHTLY with a fork until the mixture holds together and you can form a ball of dough with your hands. On a floured smooth surface, roll out the pie crust until it is a circle that is about 2" larger than the pie pan. Carefully lift the crust into the pie pan and press it in lightly to fit. With scissors or a knife, cut the pie crust edge uniformly one to one and a half inches longer than the edge of the pan. Fold the excess crust under and crimp or flute the edges.

9" double pie shell

Servings:	1 pie	2 pies	3 pies	4 pies	5 pies	6 pies
Ingredients:						
flour	2½ C.	5 C.	7½ C.	10 C.	12½ C.	15 C.
salt	½ t.	1 t.	1½ t.	2 t.	2½ t.	1 T.
shortening	¾ C.	1½ C.	2¼ C.	3 C.	3¾ C.	4½ C.
ice water	6-7 T.	12-14 T.	18-21 T.	24-28 T.	30-35 T.	36-42 T.

Mix the dough as above, but divide the dough into two balls. Roll one ball of dough as above for the bottom crust. Fit the crust into the shell and trim the edges, but do not turn it under. Roll the top crust about the same size as the bottom. Fill the pie with fruit filling, then lift the crust onto the pie. Cut the top crust to meet the edges of the bottom crust. Turn both edges under and crimp or flute the edges. Slit the top crust with a knife in 6 places, or pierce it gently with a fork several times. Bake the pie as directed on the filling pages.

Crumb topping for single crust fruit pies:

Servings:	1 pie	2 pies	3 pies	4 pies	5 pies	6 pies
Ingredients:						
Flour	¾ C.	1½ C.	2¼ C.	3 C.	3¾ C.	4½ C.
Sugar	1 C.	2 C.	3 C.	4 C.	5 C.	6 C.
Cinnamon	½ t.	1 t.	1½ t.	2 t.	2½ t.	1 T.
Salt	¼ t.	½ t.	¾ t.	1 t.	1¼ t.	1½ t.
Cold butter	½ C.	1 C.	1½ C.	2 C.	2½ C.	3 C.

Mix dry ingredients in a bowl. Cut cold butter into small pieces, then rub the butter into the crumbs with your fingers until it is well mixed and crumbly. Sprinkle over single crust fruit pies and bake as directed.

Recipe: Easy Freezer Pie Fillings

Apple pie filling:

Servings:	1 pie	2 pies	3 pies	4 pies	5 pies	6 pies
Ingredients						
Sugar	1 C.	2 C.	3 C.	4 C.	5 C.	6 C.
Salt	½ t.	1 t.	1½ t.	2 t.	2½ t.	1 T.
Cinnamon	1 t.	2 t.	1 T.	1T. + 1 t.	1T. + 2 t.	2 T.
Nutmeg	½ t.	1 t.	1½ t.	2 t.	2½ t.	1 T.
Flour	1 ½ T.	3 T.	4½ T.	6 T.	7½ T.	9 T.
Butter/margarine	2 T.	4 T.	6 T.	8 T.	10 T.	12 T.
Cooking apples; peeled and sliced	4 C.	8 C.	12 C.	16 C.	20 C.	24 C.
Lemon juice	¼ C.	½ C.	¾ C.	1 C.	1¼ C.	1½ C.

Mix sugar, salt, cinnamon, nutmeg, and flour in a small bowl. With a fork, blend butter into sugar mixture until it is crumbly. Place the lemon juice in a large bowl. As you peel and slice the apples, place them in the lemon juice and toss to coat well. When all apples have been coated with the lemon juice, pour apple slices into a colander and drain well. In a large bowl, mix drained apple slices and sugar mixture. Put apple mixture in a labeled freezer bag or container. Remove excess air, seal and freeze.

Cherry pie filling:

Servings:	1 pie	2 pies	3 pies	4 pies	5 pies	6 pies
Ingredients:						
Sugar	1 C.	2 C.	3 C.	4 C.	5 C.	6 C.
Flour	3 T.	¼C. + 2T.	½C. + 1 T.	¾ C.	¾C. + 3T.	1 C. + 2T.
Salt	1/8 t.	¼ t.	3/8 t.	½ t.	1/2t.+1/8t.	¾ t.
Butter/margarine	2 T.	4 T.	6 T.	8 T.	10 T.	12 T.
Sour pie cherries (Fresh, frozen*, or canned and drained)	4 C.	8 C.	12 C.	16 C.	20 C.	24 C.

In a large bowl, mix sugar, flour, and salt. With a fork, mix in butter until it is crumbly. Stir in pie cherries, stirring to coat well. Pour cherry mixture into a labeled freezer bag or container. Remove excess air, seal and freeze.

To Serve, Thaw filling, pour into pie shell, and seal top crust or sprinkle with crumbs. Bake at 425° for 10 minutes, then reduce heat to 350°. Bake for 30-40 minutes until browned and bubbly.
* If starting with frozen fruit, do not thaw, and increase the measurement of fruit by 1 cup.

Pumpkin pie filling:
Homemade pumpkin pie filling freezes well. Follow the directions for your favorite pumpkin pie filling and pour it into a labeled 1-gallon freezer bag. Remove excess air, seal and freeze.
To Serve: Thaw completely, pour into a single pie crust and bake as usual.

Recipe: Sparkling Fruit Splash

Serves: (8 oz.)	6	12	18	24	30	36
Ingredients:						
Frozen fruit juice concentrate, canned	12 oz.	24 oz.	36 oz.	48 oz.	60 oz.	72 oz.
Club soda, chilled	36 oz.	72 oz.	108 oz.	144 oz.	180 oz.	216 oz.

To Serve:

Option 1: Fill a glass or goblet a little less than ¼ full of frozen or thawed fruit juice concentrate. Fill slowly with chilled club soda. When the fizzing has died down a little, give the glass a little swirl with a spoon.

Option 2: Pour thawed fruit juice concentrate into a gallon pitcher. Very slowly pour in the chilled club soda. Stir slowly a couple of times until mixed.

Comments: This recipe will produce a beverage very similar to those expensive fruit drinks in bottles that look like champagne. In our experience, this beverage is a hit with the adults as well as children. Try white grape or apple juice concentrate to serve with turkey meals, blue grape juice concentrate with beef meals, and cherry juice concentrate with pork. Apple or orange juice concentrates make for a very festive breakfast or brunch beverage.

Storage Time:
Frozen fruit juice concentrates: Refrigerator (40°) 2-3 days, Freezer: 6 months

30 DAY GOURMET ORDER FORM

Send to: P.O. Box 272, Brownsburg, IN 46112
Fax to: 1-317-852-1946
Call toll-free: 1-800-9-MANUAL
Website: www.30daygourmet.com

The FREEZER COOKING MANUAL from 30 DAY GOURMET $14.95

Our comprehensive system for assembling and freezing 4-6 weeks' worth of tasty, nutritious entrees, side dishes and snacks in an easy-to-follow format. Includes:

- ❖ Time Saving Worksheets
- ❖ Step-By-Step Instructions
- ❖ 60+ Delicious Recipes
- ❖ Cooking Tips & Practical Money-Saving Advice
- ❖ 100+ Equivalents
- ❖ Master Mixes
- ❖ 20+ Easy Sauces & Marinades
- ❖ Indispensable Tally Sheet
- ❖ Nutritious Snacks
- ❖ 20 Photos

30 DAY GOURMET COOKING APRONS $19.95

- ❖ Style 1: "30 DAY GOURMET" logo
- ❖ Style 2: "Great Cooks Do It Once-A-Month" with 30 Day Gourmet logo

Color: Royal Blue with dark yellow print   *Adjustable Neck Strap*
Material: Durable poly/ cotton, washable   *Size: 30" X 36" (knee length)*

30 DAY GOURMET HOLIDAY COOKING BOOK $7.95

Our system for assembling and freezing your entire holiday meal. No more all night cooking. Make dinner when you have the time! Out traditional feasts serve 6 – 36 guests without the traditional hassle. Includes:

- ❖ Easy Step-By-Step Instructions
- ❖ 26 Delicious recipes to feed 6-36 guests
- ❖ Freezing and Cooking Tips
- ❖ Low-fat Alternatives

30 DAY GOURMET *LIVE* VIDEO $19.95

90 minute seminar/teaching video full of fun and great information. Nanci and Tara walk you step-by-step through 30 Day Gourmet plan. It covers:

- ❖ Choosing Recipes
- ❖ Assembling in Quantity
- ❖ Buddy System Benefits
- ❖ Shopping Smart
- ❖ Freezing for Great Results

30 DAY GOURMET CONSULTANT KIT $99.95

All you need to host a successful seminar about 30 Day Gourmet cooking. Includes:

- ❖ 2 Freezer Cooking Manuals
- ❖ "Great Cooks Do It Once A Month" Apron
- ❖ 90 Minute Seminar/Teaching Video
- ❖ Comprehensive Consultant Planner
- ❖ 5 Seminar Posters
- ❖ Folder Full of Supplies & Publicity Helps
- ❖ 2 Holiday Cooking Books
- ❖ "30 Day Gourmet Apron" (Personally Monogrammed)
- ❖ Book Display Easel
- ❖ 25 Recipe/Price Sheets
- ❖ 25 Postcard Invitations
- ❖ 25 Customer Bags

PACKAGE DEALS:

Package Deal #1 – Two Manuals   **$27.95 (save $2.00)**
Package Deal #2 – Manual & Holiday Book   **$19.95 (save $3.00)**
Package Deal #3 - Manual, Holiday Book, & Apron **$34.95 (save $8.00)**

BULK ORDERS:

10+ Freezer Cooking Manuals at 50%   **$7.50 each**
10+ Holiday Cooking Books at 50%   **$4.00 each**
5+ Videos at 50%   **$10.00 each**
5+ Aprons at 40%   **$12.00 each**

over for order form

Please fill out completely and send or fax to us.

Date:	
Customer Name:	
Address:	
City: State: Zip Code:	

Telephone Number: Home (**)** _____ - _____

                          Work (_____**)**_____ - _____

E-mail address:

QTY	DESCRIPTION	PRICE	TOTAL
	Pkg. 1 – 2 Manuals (save $2.00)	$27.95	
	Pkg. 2 – Manual & Holiday Book (save $3.00)	$19.95	
	Pkg. 3 – Manual, Holiday Book, & Apron (save $8.00) Which apron? _____	$34.95	
	30 Day Gourmet Cooking Manual	$14.95	
	Each Additional Manual	$12.95	
	30 Day Gourmet Holiday Book	$7.95	
	Apron – "Great Cooks Do It Once A Month"	$19.95	
	Apron – "30 Day Gourmet"	$19.95	
	Video	$19.95	
	Consultant Kit	$99.95	

Priority Mail	2-3 days	Standard Mail	7-10 days	SUB TOTAL	
Purchase	Rate	Purchase	Rate	Priority Mail or	
Up to $23.95	$5.00	Up to $18.95	$3.00	Standard Mail	
$24.00-$35.95	$6.00	$19.00-$39.95	$4.00	5% Tax (IN only)	
$36.00-$47.95	$7.00	$40.00-$59.95	$5.00		
$48.00 & up	15%	$60.00 & up	10%	TOTAL	

Prices subject to change without notice.

Payment Method: ☐ **Master Card**   ☐**Visa**   ☐**Discover**   ☐**AmEx**
                             ☐ **Personal Check**   ☐**Money Order**

Card Number: ☐☐☐☐ - ☐☐☐☐ - ☐☐☐☐ - ☐☐☐☐

Expiration Date: __ _/ __ _   Cardholder Signature: _____

How did you hear about 30 Day Gourmet? _____

Send to: P.O. Box 272, Brownsburg, IN 46112
Fax to: 1-317-852-1946
Call toll-free: 1-800-9-MANUAL
Website: www.30daygourmet.com